*How to
Order
and
Eat in
Chinese*

Buwei Yang Chao

HOW TO ORDER AND EAT IN CHINESE

Vintage Books
A Division of Random House
New York

First Vintage Books Edition, April 1974

Copyright © 1974 by Buwei Yang Chao

All rights reserved under International and Pan-American Copyright Conventions. Published in the United States by Random House, Inc., New York and simultaneously in Canada by Random House of Canada Limited, Toronto.

Library of Congress Cataloging in Publication Data

Chao, Pu-wei (Yang), 1889–
    How to order and eat in Chinese.
    1. Cookery, Chinese. 2. Gastronomy. 3. Food—Dictionaries—Chinese. 4. Chinese language—Dictionaries—English. I. Title.
TX641.C48 642'.5 73–17288
ISBN 0–394–71983–2

Book Design by Charlotte Staub
Manufactured in the United States of America

PREFACE

Since the publication of my *How to Cook and Eat in Chinese*, I have received numerous inquiries, from people who do not cook or have no time to cook, about how to order meals in Chinese restaurants. I did throw out some hints here and there about such matters in my cookbook, *How to Cook and Eat in Chinese*, but have never given any overall account of those ideas. This little book is designed for such a purpose. I shall describe briefly the meal systems one finds in China, but my primary purpose here is to tell how to order and eat in Chinese *in America*.

As usual, I write in Chinese and one of my daughters translates it into English. This time it was my third daughter, Lensey Namioka, who

did the translation, with the usual irrelevant foot-
notes by my husband.

Buwei Yang Chao

Berkeley, California
January 1973

CONTENTS

How to
Order
and
Eat in
Chinese

INTRODUCTION

China, with its long history, its vast area, and its great population, enjoys an extremely varied cuisine. Within the large Chinese family, special attention has always been paid to the preparation of food. In fact, written recipes existed more than two thousand years ago.

Difficulties of communication made uniform cuisine impossible in the old days, and regional differences in prosperity and local produce led to regional differences in taste. Now that transportation has improved by means of trains and airplanes, these regional styles of cooking can be known and appreciated by the whole country and still have the individualities of those regions.

Special tastes and styles came about in other ways. The Chinese have always maintained that food supply is dependent half on nature and half on human industry. Anything not actually poisonous was considered edible. In fact, with some poisonous substances, people investigated ways to render them harmless and developed a special taste for them.

Still other tastes developed from the need for food preservation. Before the days of canning and refrigeration, food was prepared by salting and air-drying.* People began to enjoy food treated with these methods, thus making a virtue of necessity. Now we have canned and frozen foods, but they do not taste the same as food salted and air-dried, and some people have not abandoned the old methods of preservation.

The Chinese also have techniques for dealing with germs. For instance, they avoid eating salads made with raw foodstuffs during hot weather. The cooking method employed is either prolonged simmering or stir-frying in hot oil. The temperature reached is certainly high enough to kill all bacteria, and sterilization naturally results. People jokingly say that when fried even the heads of flies can be eaten.

Another preservation technique is to let the food rot and then marinate it in brine and strong liquor for a few months before eating. Food treated in this way becomes germ-free as well as tasty. A good example is fermented bean curd, which is comparable to cheese in the Western countries.

The tastes and cooking techniques in China have not changed basically from those of the old

* See *How to Cook and Eat in Chinese* (Vintage Books, 1972), Chapter 9.

days. The ingredients, now as then, depend on their availability. But as I have said elsewhere, Chinese cooking is very flexible and adapts itself well to changing conditions, and unlike Western cooking, it tends to follow relatively definite procedures.

At the present moment, the breaking down of barriers between China and the West has led to a great interest in Chinese food. People like to read about the banquets given by the Chinese to their distinguished visitors, and they study the menus at those affairs with keen interest. Unfortunately, many of the famous and rare dishes served are not easy for the ordinary housewife to prepare at home. For one thing, the ingredients required are hard to obtain, and for another, some of the dishes will not come out well when cooked in small quantities. You might slave over them for a long time and then find the results disappointing. For example, such things as shark's fins, sea cucumber, and bird's nest have little taste in themselves. You have to add chicken, duck, pork, or other ingredients to provide flavor. It is much better to order these dishes in restaurants. There they have them already prepared in large quantities, and the necessary soup stock is always at hand. It is less expensive than preparing them in small quantities at home. One exception is bird's nest. This is relatively simple to prepare and can be cooked in either large or small quantities.*

One good reason why Chinese cooking is never monotonous is that the Chinese make a point of eating seasonal foods. Certain foods are naturally abundant at certain times of the year, and this is

* See *How to Cook and Eat in Chinese*, pp. 169–70.

what Confucius meant when he said, "Eat not what is not in season." Food that has been frozen or canned is not considered to be of top quality.

Before I go on to talk about ordering in Chinese restaurants, I should like to talk about the regional differences in cooking. As I have said, the country is vast and transportation was difficult in the past. Consequently the people in each locality were able to maintain their individual cuisines without being influenced by those of other localities. In Chinese restaurants abroad which offer a mixture of cuisines, including both Northern and Southern, you can ask whether such and such a dish is predominantly salty or sweet or spicy-hot in taste. Each of the regional cuisines is completely different, both in flavoring and in ingredients. (The situation is different in most Western countries, where the cooking is relatively uniform and varies from region to region only in minor details.)

I will treat the main Chinese regional cuisines, in special chapters. Since I obviously cannot describe all the small regional differences, I shall divide the country into four large sections. Cantonese, Northern, Szechwan, and Southern. What I consider Northern includes the provinces Shantung, Honan, and Hopeh, where, of course, Peking is situated. Southern would be the areas in the Yangtze basin, not including Szechwan, which is the third main category.

Actually, the cuisine that is most commonly encountered in Chinese restaurants outside of China is that of Canton. Strictly speaking, it is not part of the so-called Southern cooking of the Yangtze area. Cantonese cooking was originally one of the major Chinese cuisines. However, in an effort to accommodate Western tastes, many Cantonese restaurants abroad have debased their cooking. As a result, many people think of Cantonese or even all Chinese food as merely chop suey—which is an unfortunate misunderstanding. Meanwhile, Northern and Szechwan food are becoming more and more popular abroad.

I shall describe how to distinguish and order the various kinds of food in Chinese restaurants. I shall also add a few words on preparing those dishes at home for the family or for company. But first a word about the types of meals in China and Chinese meals abroad.

1

MEALS
AND
BETWEEN
MEALS

In China, where I grew up, we ate in between meals as well as at meals, and we still do the same in America. We also spoke of three meals a day. I shall first describe briefly the types of meals actually eaten in China as a background and then you can compare the Chinese meals one finds in this country. In most parts of China one eats a light breakfast, such as congee, which is a thin kind of boiled rice, some "small dishes" of salted vegetables, "hundred-year eggs," etc., as condiments, with or without (fried or scrambled) eggs, sometimes plus fried hollow long doughnuts and/or sesame-seed biscuits. Then there will be two main meals, usually dinner at noon and supper at night, with rice and accompanying dishes. I say accompanying dishes, because the essential part of a meal is rice—so much so, that the word *fan* means ambiguously either (cooked) rice or a meal, where everything else at the table is secondary, or rice-chasers. A child is said to be good when he eats much rice and not so much of the other things for giving taste to the rice. This is therefore the opposite of the idea in Western countries, where the main course, such as a roast, is the *fan,* while all other things, including rice and potatoes, are accompaniments. One important consequence of this is that most Chinese dishes tend to be more highly seasoned than would be suitable for eating as a main dish in an American-style dinner. The Cantonese word for the non-grain dishes is in fact *soong,* literally "send," that is, that with which to send down the rice.

In the Canton region and some other parts of China, ordinary working people ate two meals a day, one in the middle of the morning and the other in late afternoon. Then, the better-to-do in those places, who had time and money, would have an early light breakfast, a noontime tea, and a midnight snack. That is how the system of teas or *tim-sam* became such an important institution in areas like the Cantonese region.

In central China, including Anhwei (the province of my ancestors), breakfast, like the other two meals, also has regular boiled rice instead of the thin watery kind. Thus, one eats three square meals a day.

In the north, where more wheat is grown than rice, steamed breads with wheat flour are used instead of rice, but the expression referring to a meal is still *fan*.

As for vegetables, they are, for hygienic reasons, either eaten cooked or at least parboiled and cooked if used in a salad.

One never eats sweet pastry or fruits except at banquets. One eats them only between meals. Unlike daily meals, with all dishes served on the table simultaneously, a banquet consists of dishes following one after another. There is usually a sweet dish or two served in the middle as interludes for variety.

Tea is normally not served at meals but only between meals. For the liquid accompanying meals, there is congee (thin boiled rice) for breakfast and soup at the other meals. Instead of being served at the beginning, soup is on the table from beginning to end, like water in American meals.

One important feature of Chinese meals is the practice of community eating—that is, dishes are served (whether simultaneously at informal meals or successively at a formal dinner), in the center of the table and everybody helps himself using chopsticks or spoons, directly from the serving bowls; only the rice bowls are served individually.

So much for eating in the style of old China. Eating Chinese food in the Chinatowns in America or in Americanized Chinese homes—which is our chief concern here—is rather different. Many Chinese homes in America just eat American breakfasts, with orange juice, toast and what not, though I personally would still want my Chinese salty tidbits to chase down my eggs. As for fried hollow doughnuts and sesame-sprinkled hot biscuits, as well as congee (called *chuk,* pronounced "joke" with a jerk), which can be found in some places in the New York and San Francisco areas, instead of being served at breakfast, they are often week-end noontime specialties or midnight snacks.

As variations of the regular meals with rice and accompanying foods, we have special festive dishes. There is the *Lohan Chai,* or Arhat's Feast, consist-ing of a great variety of vegetables to delight those who must eat only vegetarian food for religious or health reasons. But this dish is also used as one of the courses at a big dinner. Another party dish is the fire-pot, or chafing dish Chinese style. Rinsed Lamb is especially good prepared this way. Here a big pot of soup is set boiling at the center of the table. Each guest "rinses" briefly a thinly sliced piece of lamb in the broth and then puts it into his own bowl of seasoning to cool and flavor before eating. Toward the end, various vegetables are placed in the pot for a soup to end the meal. An-other special dish is Peking Duck, or crisp-skin duck. This is never roasted at home and is always eaten in a restaurant. It is said that for some years the duck used at the famous Pienyi Fang Restau-rant outside the Shunchih Gate in Peking was really Long Island duck raised in China. Another story has it that the Long Island duck is of Chinese origin. Anyway, the way the dish is done is a hun-dred percent Chinese.

The occasion for eating another special food is the crab party. In the Shanghai region, and some-times in the northern provinces, when fresh-water crabs are in season, a family often has a big party eating plain boiled crabs shelled at the table and eaten with vinegar and ginger bits, two or three crabs to each person, depending upon size (of crab or person). As crabs are traditionally believed to be "cold" in nature, one usually drinks hot ginger brown sugar water, to "take off the coldness." Whatever the medicinal value, it always gives a nice contrast in taste. The feeling of being full after a crab party is illusory, however, and one usually follows it, either immediately or after a while, with a light supper of congee and small dishes.

To come to the main meals one finds in American Chinese restaurants, much concession has been made to American eating customs. Each person has a plate from which he eats, and if the hostess is not sure that her American guests know how to handle chopsticks she sometimes asks for forks to be supplied in addition, although Chinese dishes are prepared in such a way that a knife should never be necessary. Dishes are served by each person or by the hostess into the individual plates. But soup is served in individual bowls, and usually at the beginning of the meal according to American custom. Contrary to Chinese custom, tea is usually served just like water, instead of before or after the meal away from the table. Even cold water is served in some American Chinese restaurants, especially when no table wine is served. Some sweets are served at the end—again an American custom—in the form of Eight-Jewel Rice, etc., often followed by fortune cookies, something quite unknown in China.

2

CHINESE TABLE MANNERS

In China an invitation dinner begins with a fight over precedence or, rather, over yielding precedence: who should enter the dining room first, who should be seated at the head of the table, who should be next, and so on. After a fittingly long deadlock at such moments, some senior member of the party will quote the Chinese saying, "Better obedience than deference," and starts in first and gets the party going. The guest of honor is seated farthest inside the room and the host or hostess sits with his or her back toward the door through which the waiter comes to serve the dishes. In mixed parties couples are seated together by pairs.

This is the practice I have followed all these years in America. The American practice of separating couples at tables is based on the theory that everybody can speak to somebody other than a spouse either on the right or on the left. But my own theory is that at table the conversation should be general, so that anybody can speak to anybody else. That is why I never like the big-table Chinese dinners, whether formal or informal, where dishes will have to be passed unless suitably repeated a few seats along the long table.

You are all familiar with chopsticks. Those of you who have mastered their use know that with the food already bite-size, chopsticks are much more convenient than knives and forks, especially if you have to shift the fork constantly from the left hand to the right.

Since many Americans who go to Chinese restaurants have already mastered the use of chopsticks, it may be a compliment to the customers when the management does not provide forks unless asked for. Once, when I said that with chopsticks one can eat anything, someone asked, "How about steak?" I said, "Of course—you just pick up the steak and bite morsels from it. If you can't do that, then the steak isn't tender enough to eat."

Because of the general practice of community eating, the plates are very small, as each person is expected to take a small portion at a time. If one takes several things from each common dish and piles them up on his own dish, it looks like hoarding to the Chinese eye. Some families and restaurants in America follow the practice of using serving spoons and serving chopsticks in addition to the

individual chopsticks. But after having lived in
America for forty years off and on, I am still not used
to changing my chopsticks all the time. I forget to
change chopsticks and absent-mindedly eat with the
serving ones. Then, when I remember that I have
to change chopsticks, I would use my own chopsticks to serve my neighbors. Speaking as a doctor,
I find it quite hygienic to take pieces of food from
the common dish with my own chopsticks—especially as they are normally already cut up and
merely need to be picked up. If the food is a whole
piece, such as a large fish or a shoulder of beef,
the hostess can first cut it up with a serving spoon
or chopsticks into convenient-sized pieces for each
guest to pick up. One reason I prefer to let the
guests choose their own morsels is that one cannot
tell their preferences. For instance, I like fish heads
and chicken wings and would miss what is to me
the best part of a dish if I am served the fillet or the
breast. As for soups, most Chinese families and
restaurants are so Americanized that they serve
soup in individual bowls, and even, contrary to
traditional Chinese practice, at the beginning of
the meal. While it is not considered good manners
to smack one's lips while eating, it is perfectly all
right to suck one's hot soup from a spoon or a bowl
to cool the temperature and diffuse the flavor. Before I came to America, I had been taught in a
missionary school that it was bad manners to suck
soup. But since then I hesitate less about eating my
soup audibly, as I have noticed that Americans often
blow their noses in public, which sounds much
louder and less appetizing than slurping one's soup.

In Chinese usage one not only drinks soup, one

even, in a sense, drinks rice. When a bowl of rice is getting low, it is hard to fish out the last grains with chopsticks, and only small children eat rice with a spoon. So the only effective way of getting at it is to lift the bowl in a drinking position and shovel the rice in with chopsticks, down to the last grain. Why must one eat one's rice to the last grain? Because rice is the fruit of the toil of other people and it is considered sinful to waste any of it. This teaching has been so ingrained in me that to this day I would hesitate to discard any rice, although I don't mind throwing away any amount of meat or vegetables. When a colleague of my husband's at Academia Sinica came to America, he sometimes had to eat things from a plate, of course, but when there was rice on it, he would put the plate against his mouth and shove in the rice so that not one grain would be left and wasted. In China it is said that if a child leaves any rice in the bowl, his future mate will have as many pock marks on the face as the grains left uneaten. Since I still have three or four marks from an early siege of smallpox, my husband must have left a few grains of rice in his bowl when he was a child.

One "new" invention that has simplified serving Chinese food at the table is the lazy Susan. I put quotes around "new" because long before Chinese restaurants in America started to use the lazy Susan, my father contrived a homemade turntable under a hole in the center of the table, also supported on ball bearings, which could be turned under the table by the host, so as to put the various dishes within reach of the guests. In the case of a Chinese fire-pot, which usually stands very high on the table, this device could be lowered, so as to make the pot nearly flush with the table and thus more accessible to everybody. In America, when a lazy Susan is used, I usually tell the waiter to place the dishes near the edge so that they can be reached more easily. But since the hostess is expected to be solicitous to the guests and the guests want to be polite, everybody still tends to serve things to everybody else across the table and the lazy Susan just lazies around and loses its real function. This happens with both American and Chinese guests and I usually urge everybody by repeating the now hackneyed phrase: "Better obedience than deference."

Problems are, of course, simplified when you go to an American Chinese restaurant with a Chinese hostess or guest. But if you go without one, the thing is to give assurance that it is the real Chinese food that is desired. A smattering of a few words (whether in Mandarin or in Cantonese, see Chapter 11) would, of course, impress the waiters. Another thing is to ask for chopsticks instead of, or at least in addition to, knife and fork. The use of a bilingual menu, which is very common nowadays, may be of help. But don't order any form of chop suey or chow mein with noodles—unless you really like it. A restaurant with the latter on the menu is not likely to be very Chinese anyway.

3

TYPES OF DISHES AND SEASONINGS

Since this is a book for eaters, I shall go into matters of cooking and seasoning only when it concerns the eaters. As I noted before, one does not find seasonings on the table—except vinegar and ginger for special crab parties and the like—because salt and pepper and soy sauce on the table would be a reflection on the judgment of the chef. In the Chinese restaurants in this country, however, it is customary to have a set of various kinds of seasonings, such as soy sauce and mustard, on the table to suit the individual customers. It always amuses me when a friend of mine, a famous biochemist, puts soy sauce on his rice; when we invite him to our house I always put a bottle of it in front of him. In general, it is a good idea to taste the food first before adding any seasoning and possibly ruining what the cook has prepared for us.

What one finds in American Chinese restaurants, served either individually in small compartmentalized dishes or in bottles at the center of the table are usually soy sauce and mustard; and sometimes there will also be vinegar, oyster sauce, hot sauce, and bean paste (for roast duck).

Soy sauce is well known and available at many of the general groceries. Somewhat more difficult to find in stores are thicker sauces often called bean paste, which are used for certain dishes. The general name in Chinese is *chiang*, 4th tone, as distinct from *chiang yu* for ordinary soy sauce. There are several varieties with different names and slightly different ingredients. Some are made from fermented wheat flour and some from seafood, whence the Cantonese term *hoiseen cheung*, "sea-flavor sauce." Although these varieties do not taste exactly alike, their function is the same, namely, as a thick binder sauce for roasts and sometimes for boiled noodles.

Another brown sauce, found in many Cantonese dishes, is oyster sauce, or *ho-yau*. Properly, it is made from dried oysters, but most bottled oyster sauce is made from oyster juice and is darkened with caramel. In taste, a dish containing oyster sauce is not noticeably "fishy." Oyster sauce is thicker than soy sauce, but thinner than *chiang*, or bean paste. Of the other seasonings and spices, I might mention coriander, or Chinese parsley, which some do not like and others like very much.*

---

* I had to learn to like it after having to spit it out the first time I ate it.—Y.R.C.

Szechwan pepper, or fagara, is more often used in cooking than as table garnish.*

To take up the types of dishes in terms of the methods of cooking, the most important are the red-cooked, clear-simmered, dry-cooked, stir-fried, steamed, roasted, and pot-stewed dishes.

RED-COOKED

A dish is red-cooked if it contains soy sauce and a small amount of water, and is stewed in a covered pot over a slow fire. Such a dish is served more often at home than in a restaurant because it does not require a great deal of cooking skill, and also because the food tends to boil down quite a bit and the restaurants feel they have less to show for what they have put in.

CLEAR SIMMERING

This method consists of simmering the food in water over a small fire. It is called clear because very little seasoning is put in: some salt and perhaps a slice or two of ginger root and a dash of wine. The resulting broth is an important part of the dish and is served as a soup.

DRY-COOKING

With this method the food is cooked over a medium fire with seasonings including soy sauce, wine, scallions, garlic, and so on, with little or no water until the liquid is almost dry. The result is a rather strongly seasoned dish.

* For greater detail for cooking purposes I refer the reader to my *How to Cook* book, p. 29.

STIR-FRYING

In this case the food is cut up fine, diced, shredded, or sliced into thin pieces. Then it is sautéed in a pan with hot oil over a big fire and stirred constantly. A *wok* (an iron pan hemispherical in shape) would be ideal for this purpose if you happen to have a Chinese type of stove, with a big hole on top of the range for the pan to rest on. But even without such a stove a wok can be used because woks are now sold in American stores with a heavy ring on which they can rest.

(The verb "to stir-fry," which I coined and used in my *How to Cook and Eat in Chinese,* has now been generally adopted and is found in a number of cookbooks.)

STEAMING

A special Chinese steamer is best for this purpose. It consists of a big pot for boiling water, with one or more perforated layers to rest over it. Steamed breads are made this way, and the result is perfect for people who do not like the crusts on bread. The method is also used for some fish and chicken dishes. It is usually advisable to put a layer of thin gauze or even some lettuce leaves under the food, to keep it from sticking to the steaming tier.

ROASTING

In home cooking the Chinese do not do much roasting because it needs special equipment. They prefer to have roast duck, roast pig, etc., in restaurants.

LU, or POT-STEWED

Lu-tzu means gravy and a *Lu* dish is one in which the food is boiled in a dark-brown liquid containing soy sauce, wine, sugar (optional), with seasonings like star anise. Chicken, duck, and squab are frequently fixed this way. The food is then cut up and served cold. The *lu-tzu* is kept and used over and over again, with occasional additions of water and seasonings. Over a period of time, it acquires a rich taste and full body that are impossible to duplicate quickly. I suppose packages of instant *lu-tzu* will be sold sooner or later, but like instant *au jus,* it won't be the same.

All the above forms of cooking may be done over either a gas or an electric stove, though traditional Chinese cooking was done only over coal or charcoal. But stir-frying is better done over a gas fire, as it calls for quick heating and quick stopping. When only an electric stove is available, you just have to remove the pan or wok when the dish is done.

4

THE INFORMAL DINNER

Apart from special parties, regular Chinese dinners—whether ordered in a restaurant or prepared at home—may be classified into two main categories: informal dinners and banquets (I am using the term "banquet" in the sense of a full table for a definite occasion and a certain formality of structure).

"The informal dinner" is literally, in Chinese, an ordinary family meal, but it is not just for members of the family, nor is it confined to home cooking. For example, you can say to a few friends, "Let's go and have an informal meal somewhere." You can choose either a large well-known restaurant or a small intimate place. The important thing is to tell the restaurant as soon as you arrive that you want an informal dinner. Then they will know that you do not want a banquet and will hand you the menu of dishes that can be served fairly promptly.

Some small restaurants serve only informal dinners. They do not aim at having a wide range, but they will have a few dishes or even just one specialty which they do well. Some of the greatest pleasures of eating Chinese food come from seeking out those small restaurants and testing the specialties of the house. It does not mean, of course, that the other dishes in such places are inedible; it just means that their fame rests on those specialties. Every gourmet in China has his favorite list of little places that are unrivaled in preparing certain dishes.

EATING AN INFORMAL DINNER AT HOME OR IN A RESTAURANT

An important characteristic of the informal dinner is that the dishes arrive at the table more or less simultaneously. The stewed and dry-cooked (i.e., prepared without adding liquids) dishes are ready to serve before the diners are seated. The stir-fried dishes have to be prepared at the last minute, but even these are served in quick succession—in other words, the cook does not wait for the diners to finish each dish before putting the next one on the table. One advantage of the informal dinner is that you know what you can expect in the meal, and you can plan your attack accordingly.

When you prepare an informal dinner, you can

cook all the stewed, dry-cooked, and simmered dishes far in advance and then warm them up if necessary at the last minute. The stir-fried dishes with diced, sliced, or shredded chicken, meat, shrimps, etc., have to be cooked after the diners are seated, but the ingredients for these can all be prepared and assembled beforehand. They take only a couple of minutes to cook over a very brisk fire.

It is a fairly common occurrence in China for guests to come calling just before mealtime. This is not considered ill-bred or thoughtless. The reason is that the organization of a Chinese meal makes it easy for the hostess to feed a few extra mouths. The trick is, of course, to stretch the prepared dishes without being too obvious about it.

The hostess can simply water the soup and set a few more pairs of chopsticks. Suppose there are not enough fresh meats or vegetables to go around. In an informal dinner, there are always a few dishes that can be stretched by adding some preserved foodstuff. Those salted, dried, or fermented foods really improve the taste of many dishes, and are welcomed by family and guests alike.

Before the days of frozen and canned foods, winter was the busy time of the year for preparing and stocking up on such items as salted meats, salted fish, fermented beans, wine-cured chicken, smoked fish, etc. The cold dry air of winter is especially effective in preserving foods, which then acquire a concentrated taste and is said to be *hsien*. It is much better than the bland taste of canned foods or the watery texture of frozen food that has been thawed. Still another advantage of stretching dishes with these preserved foods is that leftovers of this sort keep much better. The word *hsien* means literally "fresh," but in terms of taste it really means the flavor of foods that have spoiled just enough to taste especially good, and not so much that they taste bad. Because the word *hsien* has acquired such a specialized meaning, you will now have to say *hsin-hsien*, literally "new fresh" when you really mean "fresh."

An informal dinner can include wine; some American Chinese serve cocktails with the cold dishes. But when drinks are served, the rice is kept back until the guests have had a chance to warm up from the drinks. At a Chinese dinner the standard wine, if it is served at all, is Shao Hsing wine, a rice wine of 22 or 23 percent alcohol, now available in most large American cities, such as New York, Boston, or San Francisco, or even Ithaca, N.Y. It tastes best when served warm.

The smaller places that primarily serve family meals do not have licenses to serve wine, and they usually provide tea to go with the meal. As I mentioned before, the Chinese do not normally drink "tea," but more of that later.) Chinese restaurants in America, however, have adopted the Western custom of serving soup first, so that diners are forced to drink quantities of tea as they get thirsty.

Americans who have visited China know that there is a white fiery liquor called Mao T'ai, the kind that Henry Kissinger tried to warn President Nixon not to *gambai* with Premier Chou En-lai. This is served at banquets and has the kick of pure gin or vodka. It is often featured at drinking parties: finger-matching games are played where the loser has to empty his cup. Since drinking, not eating, is the primary interest of these affairs, a detailed description is outside the scope of this book.

ARRANGING AN INFORMAL DINNER FOR COMPANY

Suppose we are taking a party to a restaurant for an informal dinner. The number of dishes we tell the waiter to bring will depend, of course, on the number of people present. As I have said, at an informal meal all the dishes arrive more or less simultaneously. But there are exceptions to this rule. For example, partway through the meal you may discover that there is not going to be enough food. One of the guests, who looked harmless at first, turns out to be putting away far more food than you expected. What you do then is to call the waiter over and order a few more dishes. Naturally you will ask him to recommend what the restaurant has on hand that day which is particularly fresh and good. These are dishes that they can serve fairly promptly. Nobody in your party will feel embarrassed by the necessity for ordering more; the nice thing about an informal party is that the atmosphere is really informal.

In the home, it is even easier to cope with the problem of food running out during the course of the meal. The hostess can simply run to the larder and take out some smoked fish, say, or a salted duck and arrange it on a serving dish. When food is running short, some clever hostesses use the trick of serving salty or spicy dishes that act as rice chasers. The guests will fill themselves up with bowl after bowl of rice, and leave the table with the feeling that they have had an enormous meal. Any competent hostess, of course, will always cook more than enough rice.

There is a story of a dinner where the supply of rice failed. One of the guests had finished his bowl of rice and waited impatiently for the host to notice the empty bowl and offer to refill it. Naturally, he could not commit a breach of etiquette by requesting a refill. But for some reason the host just did not notice the empty rice bowl. Finally, the guest decided to drop a subtle hint. He turned the bowl on its side so that its empty interior faced the host, and started to admire the back. "My, what a beautiful antique rice bowl!" he exclaimed. "Let me read the inscription on the bottom." The host looked unmoved at the shiny, empty interior of the bowl. Then he smiled and said, "I'm very glad you are interested in antiques. Let me show you an even better piece." He rushed to the kitchen and came back with the empty rice pot. "Here, look at the inscription on the bottom of this remarkable antique pot!"

Normally, however, the Chinese expect a surplus of rice at the end of the meal. It is not a wasteful attitude, for there are many uses for leftover rice. Fried rice,* for instance, is prepared from cooked rice, not from raw rice. The leftover dishes, too, are served again instead of being thrown away. In China, as in many American homes, there is no shame attached to serving leftover food. On the contrary, many dishes taste better when the flavors have had a chance to blend and deepen. The sort of

* The famous "flied lice," in Chinese pronunciation.—Y. R.C.

dishes that I mentioned for informal dinners, such as the stewed or simmered ones, and those using preserved foodstuffs, are always better when they make their second or third appearance on the family table. Guests, too, are not offended when they are faced with dishes that they know are leftovers.

EMERGENCY MEALS

Before ending the chapter on informal meals, I should like to say a word about emergency Chinese meals, namely the kind you buy ready-cooked from a take-out place. While the thought of eating a complete dinner from a take-out place is rather depressing, there are times when a working wife comes home late and is simply unable to start a meal from scratch. Even the worst of the Chinese take-out places provide better food than canned spaghetti or TV dinners. The better places offer a wide selection of ready-cooked chicken, duck, meat, and vegetable dishes. I have even seen ready-cooked sea-cucumber dishes. To save yourself the trouble, you can ask the cook to cut up the chicken or duck. Cantonese roast duck and roast pork are examples of food that you can buy in ready-to-eat form. In both price and quality, they are comparable to "good" dishes in a restaurant, and are not to be classed with hamburgers bought at a drive-in.

The food is brought home in paper cartons, and most of the dishes need only warming up in a pan or oven, although some can be eaten cold. A good trick when unexpected guests drop in is to order a few stir-fry dishes from a take-out place and then

dress them up by adding some meat, chicken, etc.,
that you have at home. Some places even sell ready-
made sweet and sour sauce, which you can use to
glamorize your leftovers. Only recently, when I was
unable to order anything in time for a dinner after
a Thanksgiving holiday, I ordered several ready-
made dishes from the San Francisco Chinatown
and got away with serving only a couple of my
own dishes for the company.

INEXPENSIVE LUNCHES

The most informal meal of all consists of a large
platter or bowl of rice topped with a mixture of
meat slices and greens stir-fried together. You can
get this in almost all Cantonese restaurants during
lunchtime, and it is a good way for office workers,
shopkeepers, and students to grab a quick lunch
that is tasty, nourishing, and cheap. Some of the
Mandarin cafés, especially those near college cam-
puses, have also started to offer this type of lunch.
Tea usually comes with the meal, and sometimes
even a small bowl of soup. The cost is around a
dollar, depending upon locality, and it makes a
better-balanced meal than hot dogs. Some of the
penny-counting students save half of the food to
take home and warm up for their evening meal.
They call this *Jing-ji Fan,* meaning frugal meal.

5

HOW TO ORDER AN INFORMAL MEAL

On ordering any informal meal, the first thing you tell the waiter is that it is an informal meal that you want and approximately how much money you intend to spend. The Chinese do not have the Anglo-Saxon reluctance to discuss money. Furthermore, this way you won't get an unpleasant surprise when you see the bill. Sometimes you may even get a pleasant surprise. One of my daughters told a restaurant to serve her family a $10 dinner. After a modest but well-cooked meal, she received a bill for only $8.50. The restaurant had gauged the capacity of her family and prepared the best food they had, but they simply did not have any expensive item ready that day.

As to how much money you should be prepared to spend, it is impossible for me to give
definite figures. If I say today that I pay between
$3 and $6 per person for an informal meal, this
information may be out of date by tomorrow. At
the moment, ordering an expensive item like Peking
duck may add another $18 to $20 to the total, but I
cannot promise you this price a year from now.

Moreover, prices vary considerably depending
on the locality of the restaurant. I have found that
those on the East Coast of the United States tend
to be much higher than those on the West Coast.
And, of course, you can expect to pay much more
in a place with soft lights and liveried waiters than
in a joint where the service is provided by the pro-
prietor's daughter wearing a blouse and skirt. In
this connection, I might mention that the appearance of a restaurant is independent of the tastiness
of the food served. We used to say, in Chinatown
beware of a restaurant with fancy interior decoration; it is sure to be a tourist trap. This is, however, no longer true. Many restaurants have learned
that their Western customers like atmosphere while
eating. They have abandoned their cheerfully
sleazy appearance and started remodeling. Now it
is safe to say that a nice-looking restaurant may
even serve good food!

On the question of money, I have to consider
the feelings of my Western friends. Because my
guests might be embarrassed by an open discus-
sion of money, I make it a practice to arrive in a
restaurant well in advance, even for an informal
dinner. This gives me time to make arrangements
about ordering and to settle the amount I plan to
spend.

Now that the waiter knows you want an informal meal and has an idea of your price bracket, he will hand you a menu. In a fancy establishment, this could be a huge folio of many pages decorated with silk tassles. In a humbler place with unprepossessing décor the menu could be a grubby dittoed sheet with the date on top which lists dishes available that day. A large establishment, on the other hand, prints impressive permanent menus because they can afford to keep up a permanent repertory of many dishes.

Some menus have the names of the dishes in English and Chinese side by side, while some of them have an English section, followed by a Chinese section, which is longer. Some restaurants even have separate menus in English and Chinese. If you suspect that there are items in the English version which are not in the Chinese version and vice versa, you are right: snails in pepper sauce may very well be on the Chinese menu, but not on the English one.

Sometimes a restaurant will suggest a certain group of dishes that go well together—called *ho-ts'ai* or *wo-ts'oi*,* "harmonized dishes," in Cantonese.

Suppose you don't read Chinese, but you are determined to have really authentic Chinese food. One thing you can do is to bring along a friend who can read Chinese. What happens if you get tired of always including him in your parties? You can pretend to read the Chinese menu and nod your head knowingly, then point to a few dishes at random and hope for the best. The danger is that you might

---

* Even though, as a "free" form, the Cantonese word for a dish of food is *soong*.—Y.R.C.

spoil the whole effect by holding the menu upside down. Perhaps the best thing is to insist on the Chinese menu, then have the waiter stand over you and translate the whole thing. This may take some time, but at least they will know you mean business.

The next problem is to decide how many dishes to order. For just two people, two or three dishes and a soup will probably be enough. For a party of four, you might ask for four dishes and a soup. A general rule is to order a soup plus as many dishes as there are diners. Naturally, this means that the more people there are in your party, the more variety you will have in the dinner. When the party reaches the size of eight or more people, it may be easier to reduce the number of dishes and to increase the amount in some of them. Most restaurants have two different sizes for each dish. Thus, for a party of twelve, you can order eight dishes, but with double the amount in some of them.

One nice thing about an informal meal is that the size of the party at a table is very flexible. It could be anything from two to twelve people (sometimes even fourteen, if some of them are children). This is unlike a banquet, where the number of people at each table is fixed at ten or, less frequently, twelve.

It is risky to make a hard-and-fast rule about the number of dishes to order for an informal meal. It depends not only on the size of your party, but also on the size of your guests. One guest may be a giant who eats enough for two. But as I have said before, you can always add a few dishes partway through the meal. If you end up with too much food, the restaurant will arrange to have you take it home. Since leftovers are perfectly respectable, you don't have to make any pretense about doggie bags. Most Chinese restaurants readily provide non-leaking paper cartons for the express purpose of taking home leftovers. The guest who was eating fried prawns with such gusto would be glad to take home the rest of the dish for the next day. As I said before, one of my favorite leftovers is the fish head, as many diners just leave the head alone. Once, I came home and found two heads in my carton. I called up the restaurant and asked if they had made a mistake. "No," they said, "one was your head, the other was somebody else's head."

Suppose you are in a restaurant with a fine reputation and have looked at the correct menu—are you going to have a good dinner? Not always, unfortunately. Many of my friends report that when they go to a restaurant that I have recommended, they are frequently disappointed. What really annoys them is that when I invite them to a restaurant, they get one type of dinner, but when they go by themselves a week later, they get an entirely different meal. Even some of the same dishes taste mysteriously different.

Now, having a really good meal at a Chinese restaurant is not a matter of spending huge sums of money or having a hypnotic personality. The secret is convincing first yourself, and then the management, that you really want authentic Chinese food. This is not always easy when you are not an Oriental. The waiter takes one look at your all-American face and thinks he knows just the sort of food you want.

There is some justification for the waiter's attitude. Most people take a while to adjust to unusual food, and the culture shock of eating fish tripes for the first time can be considerable. Over the years, Chinese restaurants have developed a list of "safe" dishes like Chicken with Cashews, Sweet and Sour Pork, Batter-Fried Prawns, etc. To make things easier, many places have complete dinners, each with a set price, of dishes that are chosen because they go well together. If you are not adventurous about food, you can do worse than ordering, say, Dinner #4. You don't even have to accept every dish in these dinners. If your stomach isn't up to Black Mushrooms in Oyster Sauce, which is part of Dinner #4, you can tell the waiter to substitute something else of a comparable price.

Many restaurants have found it very profitable to provide exotic atmosphere with totally unexotic fare. Some of their customers really want steak, served by sloe-eyed waitresses in slinky dresses. But since the readers of this book would not be that type of customer, I am assuming that what you want is the kind of meal that a discriminating Chinese customer gets.

You can begin by refusing knife and fork and insisting on chopsticks. Gamesmanship of this sort is not essential, however. The surest way of gaining the waiter's respect is to show him that you really know something about Chinese food. What I should like to do, then, is to tell you about some basic Chinese dishes so that your opening remarks to the waiter will establish your expertise.

As an example of an informal dinner, the following dishes are fairly representative: Sour and Hot Soup or Shrimp-Meat Rice-Toast Soup or

Winter Melon Soup (not the big half-melon soup); Beef Stirred with Scallions or Oyster Sauce, Stir-Fried Shrimp Meat or Dried-Fried Large Shrimps; Kungpao Diced Chicken (tell them if you want hot pepper added) or Walnut Diced Chicken; Sweet and Sour Spare Ribs or Ancient Old Meat; Fish, red-cooked or sweet and sour; Stir-fried greens. For dessert you can have Eight-Jewel Rice or Pull-Thread Bananas. The above is about enough for six diners.

But before you start mentioning dishes by name, you should first find out what type of restaurant you are in. If you are in a Szechwan restaurant, then naming one or two notable Szechwan dishes will immediately engage the waiter's interest. Insisting on a Szechwan dish in a Cantonese restaurant does a lot less to enhance your prestige, even though the restaurant may happen to serve that dish. But if you really have a fancy for it, you can order it a little later.

6

BANQUETS

Unlike an informal dinner, a banquet should be arranged days in advance. There are many occasions that call for banquets: a birthday, a wedding, a funeral, an expression of gratitude to someone, welcoming a visitor from out of town, a group of people honoring a mutual friend. All these are reasons for ordering a banquet served on one or more tables.

There are Shark's Fin Banquets, Sea-Cucumber Banquets, Bird's Nest Banquets, and so on. It does not mean, of course, that you eat nothing but shark's fin or bird's nest, etc. It means that such and such a notable dish is the feature of this particular banquet. When shark's fin is served, it is usual for the guests to say *"T'ai fei-shih le!* (It's been too much trouble [for you]!)."* Once a Cornell schoolmate of my husband's who knew no Chinese was invited to a banquet we gave and learned this expression from me. When he himself invited us to a shark's fin dinner he said, *T'ai fei-shih le!*

When ordering a banquet at a restaurant, the usual procedure is to give the reason for the occasion, specify the *pièce de résistance,* and mention the number of guests and the amount you plan to spend. If you happen to be very fond of some dish that you know this restaurant excels in, ask to have it included. This is also the time to tell the restaurant what dishes you want to avoid. For example, you might dislike their sweet and sour fish, or the guest of honor might be allergic to crab or believe in the folklore that crab and persimmon make a fatal combination and that turtle and *hsien-ts'ai* (*Amaranthus mangostanus*) result in something poisonous. But once I ate crabs and persimmon during one meal and did not feel sick afterward.

SHOULD YOU HAVE A BANQUET?

Obviously, if you are with a few friends just for the pleasure of each other's company, a very formal party is not what you want. A banquet is a stately affair, designed to mark an occasion. There are borderline cases, however. Your guest list may include people whom you do not know well but wish to honor especially for one reason or another. Therefore you call up the restaurant a day in advance to make sure that the dinner is an exceptional one. You may start with the idea of an informal dinner, but by the time you order eight or ten dishes, including elaborate ones like shark's fin, you are getting into the banquet price range anyway. So why not go all the way and give a full-fledged banquet?

But before you commit yourself to a banquet, you should be aware of its rather rigid structure. First of all, there is the size of the party per table. The usual size is ten people at each table, although you can stretch it to twelve by a little negotiation. Restaurants have certain sizes for the serving platters and a certain number of dishes for banquets. They also have regular prices for a Shark's Fin Banquet, a Bird's Nest Banquet, and so on, and they are reluctant to allow great variations. If you have less than ten people at a table, you are still expected to pay for a table of ten. (At a banquet, you pay for so many tables, not for so many dishes. When you say you want a $60 or an $80 banquet, you mean that you intend to pay so much *per table*.) Having fifteen people at your banquet is a miscalculation. You should have rounded up another five to fill a second table.

At a banquet the dishes arrive one at a time and the guests have to exercise almost inhuman self-control. The danger is that you may fill yourself up before the really good dishes arrive.* There is also the opposite danger that you may exercise too much restraint and realize too late that you have already passed up the choicest dishes, but this does not happen very often. Many people cannot stand the suspense of a banquet, its necessity for re-

* That's why I have always preferred, since my childhood days, to eat informal meals, since at a banquet, where one dish was served at a time, I would always eat too much of what I thought I liked best and then would have no room for the really best dishes coming later.—Y.R.C.

straint, and its interminable length. They much prefer the more relaxed informal dinner.

Most banquets start with four cold dishes, such as Sliced Ham, Dry-Fried Shrimps, Smoked Fish, "100-year-old-eggs" (salted and preserved duck's eggs), Squid Skins. In most American Chinese restaurants, these usually come on one big platter with four or more compartments. Next come the four stir-fries, one after another. Examples are Fu Yung Chicken Slices, Stir-Fried (Fresh) Shrimps, Stir-Fried Lean Pork (often replaced by beef slices nowadays), and Stir-Fried Slices of Fish. Then comes the big soup, such as the Half-Winter-Melon Soup with Sizzling Rice Toast, or Sour and Hot Soups of various kinds. The *pièce de résistance* at a banquet may be Shark's Fin, Large Sea Slug (trepang), or Peking Duck with Doilies, or Camphor Tea Duck, or Red-Cooked, Clear-Steamed, or Sweet and Sour Whole Fish. In China the climax is the four heavy dishes. Soup will appear once or twice between courses and also at the end. There are regional variations to this program, but the important thing to remember is that restaurants have a certain schedule which they follow for banquets and it is unwise to tamper with it. If you suggest a dish that is inappropriate or attempt to rearrange the order, you may give an impression of your inexperience which would have unfavorable consequences, not only for that dinner but for all future dinners at that particular restaurant.

LEAVE IT TO THE EXPERTISE
OF THE RESTAURANT

You will have gathered that my advice is to leave the arrangement of the banquet to the restaurant. After all, you picked a particular place because you trust its staff's judgment. They will decide which dishes are suitable for your occasion, what order they should appear in for maximum effect, etc.

At this point, I am assuming that you have found a place that you can trust. For many people the problem is how to find such a restaurant. Or, having heard that a certain restaurant is good, how do you make them put forth their best effort for your benefit? This is a problem not only when you order a banquet, but also when you go for an informal meal. The main thing is to gain the management's confidence that you really want and enjoy real Chinese food.

BANQUETS AT HOME

So far, I have not discussed how to hold a banquet at home. The reason is obvious. It is beyond the capabilities of an amateur cook, however talented, to marshal the long parade of dishes that go into a banquet.

Formerly, it was common for a well-to-do Chinese family to have a chef in residence. Even those people who did not have a full-time chef at home could hire one from a restaurant for the occasion of the banquet. In those days the larger restaurants had as many as half a dozen good chefs, and they could always spare one or two for outside calls.

When one hired a chef from a restaurant, it was somewhat like having a caterer. The restaurant sent all the materials for the food, and even supplied the tableware (except when the host had some particularly impressive pieces, such as antique rice bowls that he wished to show off to his guests). The chef came to the house to do the actual cooking. Unlike caterers in America, however, the restaurants did not provide services other than cooking. The host's own servants had to serve the food and clean up afterward. In addition, they were expected to cook the rice, since it was beneath the dignity of a first-class chef to cook rice.

ARRANGING DINNERS FOR LARGE GATHERINGS

I shall say just a few words about ordering Chinese dinners for large gatherings like class reunions, learned-society meetings and such. When the number of people reaches a hundred or more, there are bound to be some people with either preferences or taboos about food. This is especially true if your group is a cosmopolitan one. People of different religious and cultural backgrounds have different eating habits. Most Buddhist sects are vegetarian. In Jewish orthodoxy one eats no pork, a meat favored by the Chinese.

On one occasion, I had to arrange a banquet of thirty-eight tables for a meeting of the American Oriental Society in San Francisco. The gathering included members of all religious denominations. This meant that there were people who ate beef but no pork, those who ate pork but no beef. Some ate no animal flesh but accepted dairy products, and some ate no animal product whatever. Then there were people who ate seafood, except for shellfish, and those who shunned all seafood. And some of the people ate seafood and chicken, but not meat from hoofed animals.

A Chinese restaurant is the perfect place for such a gathering. Chinese cuisine is especially rich in ways of cooking seafood, and for the strict Buddhists, there has been a long tradition of elegant vegetarian cooking. At the dinner for the Society there were dishes to satisfy every kind of religious and cultural restrictions.

7

CANTONESE CUISINE

I shall start with Cantonese cuisine, one of the four main categories to be found among American Chinese restaurants, because the early Chinese immigrants to America were from the Canton region and they established the first Chinese restaurants in this country. Even today, the Cantonese restaurants are still by far the most numerous. Cantonese food is relatively bland in flavor and not too greasy, and thus easy on American palates. In China, Cantonese cooking is highly regarded. It is quite distinct in taste and in cooking method from that of other parts of the country.

Many Americans, however, think of chop suey

when they mention Cantonese food. There are several versions on the origin of the term "chop suey." One story has it that the Chinese envoy Li Hung-Chang was complimented on the food served at a diplomatic banquet. When asked for the recipe of a dish containing some finely chopped food, he exhibited a typical male's ignorance of kitchen matters and muttered "Chop . . . chop . . ." Then his English failed him and he added the Chinese word for "minced," namely, *suey*. This story has all the earmarks of a concocted tale.

Another version is that the early Chinese restaurants were run by laborers who had little experience in fine cooking. The mixture of celery shreds and bean sprouts swimming in cornstarch sauce was probably their attempt to seek relief from pork and beans. Perhaps the cook lacked the gall to give an honest name to this dish, and decided to coin the hybrid term "chop suey." One sign in a small San Francisco restaurant says: WE CHOP OUR OWN SUEY. In Chinese characters, the disyllable *chop suey* (*tsa sui* in Mandarin), means, literally, "miscellaneous broken."

Today no respectable Cantonese restaurant would touch chop suey with a ten-foot chopstick, but the unfortunate connotation remains. This is most unfair, because Cantonese cooking at its best is fully the equal of the other major cuisines. Where else can you get banquets featuring snake and monkey? Since many of the ingredients for these specialties are not available in Western countries—how do you get around the S.P.C.A. for your monkey banquet?—they are largely unknown outside of China (in fact, not too well-known *in* China) except by hearsay. I myself once had a dinner featuring snake soup in Canton, but its flavor was enhanced by the chicken in it.

Cantonese cooking is unexcelled in the preparation of roasts. When you take a walk in certain parts of Chinatown, you may encounter an aroma that sets your gastric juices oozing. Hanging in a cookshop, by the shades of Charles Lamb, is a whole roast pig. Its crackling skin is irresistible. Passers-by can ask the butcher to hack off a pound or two to take home, and those with little will power sometimes gobble a piece on the spot. For a special feast, you can order a whole roast pig of fifty or sixty pounds to be delivered to your home, enough meat for a hundred people. I personally find the Cantonese roast pig much tastier than that of a Hawaiian* luau.

Still another Cantonese specialty is Bird's Nest Soup. In a Cantonese restaurant you can have Bird's Nest Soup as part of an informal dinner without ordering it in advance. These restaurants know that Westerners are fond of bird's nest, and accordingly they always have some presoaked and a supply of soup stock to go with it. Northern and Szechwan restaurants, however, do not usually have bird's nest to serve at a moment's notice. They provide it only for banquets and need advance warning. Traditionally, a Bird's Nest Banquet must feature a big tureen filled with bird's nest and not just some flakes of it in the soup.

Another way the Cantonese serve bird's nest is putting it in Winter Melon Soup. This soup, made

---

* Lensey, wouldn't you say "*an* Hawaiian," since you are supposed to say *an* before an unstressed *h*?—Daddy.

But "Hawaiian" has a capital H; wouldn't that make a difference?—Lensey.

with half a melon in one whole piece, and not cut into slices, is another Cantonese specialty that you have to order a day in advance. It is a notable Cantonese dish and is usually not available in Northern or Szechwan restaurants. Even in a Cantonese restaurant, you don't order it unless you have a large party of eight or ten people, since each melon produces between ten and twenty bowls of soup. The average winter melon is comparable to a medium-sized pumpkin. The seeds are scooped out and the melon is cooked whole with the skin left on. When the flesh is tender but not too soft (or the whole thing would collapse), the hollow interior is filled with soup containing bits of chicken, ham, bird's nest, and other goodies. This is a banquet dish, and is not often seen at a casual dinner.

One Cantonese specialty familiar to many Americans and very popular is *tim-sam* (pronounced "deem sum"), literally, "dot the heart." These meat-filled pastries are eaten in the middle of the day, between 11 A.M. and 4 P.M., and never at night. You drink tea with *tim-sam,* something you don't do with a regular meal, and hence this repast is sometimes called a tea. As I have noted, the Cantonese eat two major meals a day, one in mid-morning and one in late afternoon. A poor man may stifle hunger pangs late at night with some congee (rice gruel). A well-to-do Cantonese, on the other hand, eats five meals a day. In addition to the two major meals, he eats three snacks. One of these "light" snacks is tea with *tim-sam*. Some people, especially children, enjoy this snack more than any of the regular meals.

When you enter a *tim-sam* place, you don't ask for a menu. The time for choosing is when the waiter comes around with a huge tray or cart filled with saucers, each containing three or four of the pastries, which are generally steamed, but sometimes fried or baked. You tell the waiter or point to the ones you want and he puts them down on your table. As soon as the kitchen has a new batch of the *tim-sam* ready, the waiter passes them around while they are piping hot. You stop the waiter each time he comes around until you can't eat any more. Most restaurants have between ten and twenty varieties, but few customers have the capacity to sample every variety at one sitting. To add up the bill, the waiter counts the number of saucers he left on your table. Some pastries cost more than others, and the varieties are distinguished by the different shapes of the saucers. Frenchmen would feel at home in a *tim-sam* place. The big trays with their selections are like hors d'oeuvres carts, and the saucer counting is the same as in French cafés.

Some customers like to have more than just *tim-sam*. For the Cantonese the real thing is tea only, but for others it is lunch. Most *tim-sam* cafés also serve soup, noodles, and a few modest meat and vegetable dishes. During the evening, they may have regular dinner menus. The best thing about these *tim-sam* places is that they are relatively inexpensive. You have to stuff yourself to stupefaction before your pocketbook hurts.

As mentioned before, another Cantonese snack is congee, eaten late at night, although it is eaten in the north at breakfast. It is rice boiled in a lot of water so that the consistency is like that of thick soup, though thinner than porridge. A poor man would drink the congee plain, with perhaps some pickles as accompaniment. But for those who can afford a little more, the congee is flavored with slices of meat, chicken, duck, etc. One version has slivers of raw fish. You put the fish into the congee at the table, and it is delicately cooked by the hot soup. In the larger American cities, there are Cantonese cafés specializing in rice congee and soup noodles—another popular snack at night. These places are popular with people coming from theaters, concerts, and the movies, as well as students working late. Since the soupy rice or noodles sit lightly on the stomach, they are less likely to cause Welsh rabbit nightmares.

The following is a list of some of the more typical dishes to be found in Cantonese restaurants. Occasionally these dishes will appear on menus with fanciful names, making it hard to tell what the ingredients are. When you see a name like Phoenix Foam in Celestial Sauce, you may have to ask the waiter what it contains, whether it is animal or vegetable, fish or fowl. In my list, I shall give the generic name rather than the trade name whenever possible. But some of the fanciful names are well established, and in those cases I shall put the name first, followed by a description of the ingredients. Each name will be given in Chinese characters first, then an English translation. If called for, a few remarks will be added. I shall also follow this plan in the subsequent chapters.

A. ROASTS

1. 八宝鸭   Eight-Jewel Duck (roast duck with glutinous rice and dried fruits)

2. 脆皮糯米鸭　Crisp Skin Duck in Glutinous Rice

3. 义烧　　　　Barbecued Pork

4. 烤猪　　　　Roast Pig

5. 脆皮乳鸽　　Roast Squab with Crisp Skin

6. 脆皮鸭,
　　掛炉鸭　　Roast Duck with Crisp Skin (better known as Peking Duck)

B. STIR-FRIED DISHES

1. 生炒排骨　　Stir-Fried Spare Ribs

2. 蠔油牛肉　　Beef Slices with Oyster Sauce

3. 牛肉菜心、　Beef Slices with Greens (such as bok choy or gailan)

4. 义烧菜心　　Barbecued Pork Slices with Greens

5. 水晶明虾球　Crystal-Clear Shrimp Balls

6. 豆豉明虾球　Shrimp Balls in Black Bean Sauce

7. 糟溜鱼片　　Wine Fish Slices

8. 蠔油鲍片　　Abalone Slices in Oyster Sauce

9. 蠔油冬菇　　Black Mushrooms in Oyster Sauce

10. 冬笋冬菇　　—— with Bamboo Shoots

11. 冬菇菜心　　—— with Hearts of Bok Choy

12. 奶油白菜　　Cabbage in Cream Sauce

13. 烩炸豆付　　Bean Curd ⎫

14. 炒虾仁　　　Shelled Shrimp ⎪

　　　　　　　　　　　　　　　Stir-fried with
15. 炒鱼片　　　Fish Slices　　bamboo shoots,
　　　　　　　　　　　　　　　water chestnuts,
16. 炒肉片　　　Pork Slices　　snow peas, etc.
　　　　　　　or Shreds

17. 炒鸡片　　　Chicken Slices ⎭

C. SWEET AND SOUR DISHES

1. 糖醋排骨   Sweet-Sour Spare Ribs
2. 古老肉   Ancient Old Meat (actually neither ancient nor old; pork cubes batter-fried and covered with sweet-sour sauce)
3. 糖醋魚   Sweet-Sour Fish

D. STEAMED or BOILED DISHES

1. 清蒸魚   Steamed Fish
2. 清蒸滑鸡   Steamed Whole Chicken (served cut up)
3. 油煎子鸡   Oil-Splashed Chicken (fryer boiled and then dipped in hot oil and soy sauce)
4. 香腸蒸鸡   Chicken Pieces Steamed with Sausage
5. 白切鸡   White Cut Chicken (boiled plain and served cut up, to be dipped in salt or soy sauce by diner)
6. 滷乳鴿   Squab boiled in sauce

E. RED-COOKED DISHES

1. 紅燒鴨   Red-Cooked Duck
2. 紅燒豆付   Red-Cooked Bean Curd
3. 羅漢齋   Lohan Chai, or Arhat's Feast (eighteen dried vegetables with a few fresh vegetables, stewed together)
4. 紅燒包翅   Red-Cooked Shark's Fin (Since shark's fin has little taste, it is

always cooked with meat, chicken, etc. This is such an elaborate dish that the rest of the dinner should be planned around it.)

5. 蟹黄大生翅 Shark's Fin with Crab Liver Sauce

6. 蟹肉烩鱼翅 Shark's Fin with Crab Meat

F. COLD DISHES

1. 冷拼盘　　Large Combination Cold Platter (with cold sliced meats and pickled vegetables, served at the beginning of the meal to go with wine or cocktail)

G. SOUPS

1. 清燉冬菇湯 Clear-Simmered Mushrooms

2. 燕窩湯　　Bird's Nest Soup (could be inside of a winter melon, with Crisp Rice added)

3. 冬瓜盅　　Winter Melon Soup (This combines well with the dish below)

4. 鍋巴湯　　Soup with Crisp Rice (Rice is boiled, baked dry and deep-fried. It is put into hot soup at the table, making a sizzling sound.*)

---

* An important point is that the soup should be served to each guest individually and then pieces of the hot fried rice put into it. Some waiters, from either ignorance or laziness, put the rice toast into the large bowl first, thus allowing it to become soggy; they should be forewarned not to do this.

The above list makes no claim to be complete, but it does give the representative dishes served in Cantonese restaurants in America. You will find that most of the other dishes you meet with are likely to be variations of these.

8

NORTHERN FOOD

Only recently have Americans awakened to the fact that there is a lot more to Chinese cooking than Cantonese food. Since the thaw in relations with China, there has been a tremendous surge of interest in "real" Chinese food, as opposed to the Americanized versions. Just as there was a chop-suey joint in every American town* with a population of more than 200, now there is a Mandarin café on every Main Street U.S.A.

* Once we were driving through a small town in Vermont where a coffee shop had a "chop suey sandwich" on its menu. Out of curiosity we ordered one. They just opened a can of bean sprouts and put them between pieces of bread, which, to our surprise, did not taste so bad after all.

Before going into a description of Northern food I should like to clear up a misunderstanding. Many people in America think that Mandarin cooking and Northern Chinese cooking are identical. Nowadays, any restaurant whose cook can turn out one or two non-Cantonese dishes claims to be Mandarin. This attitude is not completely unreasonable. The term "Mandarin" (which is not even Chinese in origin) was used by Europeans to denote any Chinese of the official class. Since these officials were sent to govern every part of the country, any *haute cuisine* which is of a national rather than regional character can make a fair claim to be Mandarin. At some of these Mandarin restaurants, you can get dishes from a number of different regions all in the same dinner.

The confusion of Mandarin with Northern cuisine arises from the fact that the term "Mandarin" also refers to the standard dialect of China, which is essentially that of North China. Not all speakers of Mandarin are Northern Chinese, however. The dialect of Kunming, capital of Yunnan Province, which is a city in the southwestern corner of China, is a variety of Mandarin. Similarly, your meal in a Mandarin restaurant may start with Sour-Hot Soup, a specialty of Szechwan.

The best Northern cuisine is the cooking of Shantung, Honan, and adjacent areas, while Peking, famous for its Peking Duck, is more cosmopolitan. There are differences between Shantung and Honan food, but the Northern restaurants outside of China do not usually make the distinction. In taste, Northern food is slightly saltier than that of other parts of the country. There is also a tendency to use a great deal of scallions and garlic to flavor the food.

The soil and climate of northern China are not suited to rice cultivation. People eat a lot of millet, since it is easy to grow and does not require good soil. But it is considered a poor grain, and few Northern restaurants bother to serve it. My husband has an occasional nostalgic craving for millet gruel and *wo-wo-t'ou,* a steamed bread made of cornmeal. You might try asking for *wo-wo-t'ou* in a Northern restaurant—not that there is much chance of getting it—and the cook might get overcome by nostalgia and cry on your shoulder.

Wheat is the staple of the Northern diet. Northern cooking, therefore, is noted for its breads, noodles, dumplings and pastries. While the Cantonese *tim-sam* are dainty pastries suitable for a light repast like tea, the Northern counterparts, such as *pao-tzu* (stuffed dumplings), *chiao-tzu* (wraplings), noodles, *pao-ping* (tortillas, or "doilies"), *shao-ping* (sesame-sprinkled hot biscuits), etc., are all substantial enough to form a major meal. The most proletarian form of wheat food is *ta-ping,* "big cake," a hot cake a foot and a half across by an inch thick, browned outside and soft inside, and very slightly salted. It is so filling that a proverbial lazy husband is said to have had one of these cakes put around his neck by his wife, who had to be away for a few days, but by the time she was back he was nearing starvation, because he had eaten the front half of the cake and had been too lazy to turn it around to eat the other half.

Plain noodles take the place of rice in many Northern Chinese meals. A true Northerner is happy to eat boiled noodles with nothing on them except a dash of vinegar. There are other ways of fixing noodles: chow mein, for instance, simply means fried noodles. The chow mein one finds in America is the crisp kind, not too well known in China, and when it is combined with fried (soft) noodles, you have the dish known as Chow Mein with Noodles.*

Chiao-tzu or wrapling, is a pastry made with minced meat and vegetable stuffing wrapped in thin, round pieces of unleavened dough. It is a dish that is gradually receiving its due recognition in America. Restaurants often serve them fried, in which case they are called *kuo-t'ier*, 'pot-stickers," but Northerners like best to eat them boiled and then dipped in vinegar. A *chiao-tzu* party at home is a lively occasion on which hostess and guests alike pitch in to wrap the wraplings. Everyone talks and laughs and gets in each other's way, but in spite of too many cooks, hundreds of *chiao-tzu* somehow are made and are consumed on the spot. The average person will eat a dozen to fifteen of the small Northern *chiao-tzu,* although I have witnessed people putting away as many as thirty at a sitting. In most restaurants you have to order *chiao-tzu* in advance, and you are expected to have a few side dishes. At home, *chiao-tzu* form the entire meal except for little dishes like pickles. Even soup is sometimes omitted, and the real Northerner drinks the plain broth in which the *chiao-tzu* have been

---

* My daughter Rulan Pian wrote me recently that she had noticed a sign "Soup du Jour of the Day," which she compared with Chow Mein with Noodles. The former, however, is more redundant than Chow Mein with Noodles, which in fact is not really redundant.

boiled. You can always count on a few incompetent wrappers whose *chiao-tzu* will burst apart during the cooking, thus improving the flavor of the broth.

Another type of Northern pastry party is the *pao-ping,* or doilies, dinner. *Pao-ping* are flat limp pieces of pan-baked unleavened bread, not unlike tortillas. They are from four to five inches in diameter, and when properly constructed, they tear apart into two thinner pieces. The dinner consists of *pao-ping,* together with various dishes that serve as filling: stir-fried meat shreds with bean sprouts, scrambled egg and scallion, etc. The procedure is to place a quantity of filling in the middle of the *pao-ping* and then roll it up into a tube. The result is like a lumpy homemade cigar, which you eat with your hands. If you have been greedy and used too much filling, the resulting package may disintegrate and fill your sleeves, to the amusement of your fellow diners. There is the theory that the *pao-ping* comes apart in two pieces in order to have one piece ready to wipe the juice that may trickle down your elbow.

Pao-ping is also served with the most famous Northern dish of all, the Peking (roast) Duck, sometimes called in Cantonese *K'ua-lou-Aap,* i.e., "Hang-in-oven duck," (see chapter 7, No. A6). To eat this dish, you roll up the bread with slices of duck, scallions, and bean paste. Some restaurants serve plum sauce or hoisin sauce in place of bean paste. Make sure that you include plenty of crisp skin in your package, because that is the best part of the duck.

The cost of Peking Duck makes it unlikely that a casual diner would stroll in and ask for this dish. Even if he did he is not likely to get it because it is essential to order Peking Duck a day in advance, since the skin of the duck must be dried in a special way to produce that crispness. Few restaurants can afford to have a few ducks sitting around with the skin already dried. Once treated, the duck is useless for anything else. This dish appears far more often at banquets than at informal dinners because of the advance notice necessary. If you are very fond of it or if you want to have an especially elegant informal dinner, you can call up the restaurant a day earlier. As I have said, you should expect to pay about $18 to $20 for this dish.

Peking Duck has been familiar to Americans even before the advent of Northern restaurants. A number of Cantonese restaurants have had it in their repertory for years. But in Cantonese restaurants the duck is served with layered steamed bread called *fa-chün* (or *hua-chüar*, "flowery rolls") rather than *pao-ping*. The Cantonese are skilled in doing roasts, and they sometimes do a better job with Peking Duck than even the Northern restaurants. The latter place so much emphasis on getting the skin of the duck just right that for Western tastes the meat is often underdone.

Still another Northern Chinese specialty that is gaining popularity is *pao-tzu*, a steamed dumpling with raised dough and meat filling. Cantonese *tim-sam* includes the *pao-tzu* (usually *ch'a-shiu paao*), but their version is a dainty morsel, with rather sweet dough, which you can finish in a couple of bites. The Northern version, on the other hand, is a much more hefty specimen, and one or two of them can make a lunch. In California I have seen many Mandarin drive-ins and take-out places selling *pao-tzu*. They are especially popular with impecunious students, since they cost only 15 or 20 cents each. Don't expect the really cheap ones to contain much meat, however. If you take too big a bite, you might overshoot and swallow the tiny meat filling without tasting it.

There is a Chinese story about a man who was working his way through mountains of dough in a *pao-tzu*. Eventually he came to a sign which said, "To Meat—One Mile more."* Despite such a story, a real Northern *pao-tzu* contains meat and vegetables, making a nourishing, balanced meal. You can fill yourself up very comfortably on a couple of these if you are low on funds. I wouldn't be surprised if *pao-tzu* took its place next to pizza as a part of the American way of life.

In the better Northern restaurants, you can order a refined version of *pao-tzu* with fillings of crab, shrimp, etc. One kind is *t'ang-pao* or *Hsiao-lung pao* (small-tier dumpling, No. A 6 below), which you should eat with great care, as the filling is a scalding hot liquid. When these rather small *pao-tzu* are served up in the steaming tier, I usually demonstrate for the guests by lifting one of them (the *pao-tzu* that is!) with my chopsticks and put it right on my spoon, to keep the juice from being lost if put on a plate. Although not very expensive, *t'ang-pao* usually has to be ordered in advance.

Next to pork, the commonest form of meat used in north China is lamb or mutton. Its characteristic tang repels some Chinese from other parts of the

---

* The Chinese version is "three *li*," one *li* being about one-third of a mile.

country, and a good test for identifying a Northerner is to observe his reaction to lamb: if he shies away from it, he is not a true Northerner born and bred. You might call this a way to separate the sheep from the goats.

Rinsed Lamb, among other notable lamb dishes, has the status of an institution. It is a Northern Chinese version of Fondue Bourguignonne. Using chopsticks, you dip paper-thin slices of lamb into a pot of broth that is set to boil on the table. Without relaxing your grip, you rinse it around until the meat is just barely cooked. Then you quickly lift it out and dip it into a bowl of sauce which you have mixed to your own taste. Most diners favor a mixture of sesame paste, soy sauce, shrimp oil, and chopped scallions. By the time the broth has rinsed many pieces of lamb, it has become a very flavorous soup. Then you add vegetables and noodles to it and finish off the meal in an orgy of slurping. An alternative procedure is to put a lot of slices of lamb in the broth then pick out those that look the right color. This is sometimes quicker, but less orderly.

If you have Rinsed Lamb in a restaurant, you are not expected to order anything else except some cold dishes (see list below). The traditional accompaniments, such as *shao-ping* (sesame biscuits), are served automatically. Peking boasts a number of famous Rinsed Lamb restaurants. However, there are few restaurants outside of China that serve it, although other forms of Fire-Pots (i.e., dishes cooked at the table) are to be found in Northern and Cantonese restaurants in America.

Chinese hostesses in America like to serve Rinsed Lamb when they entertain at home. They find it very convenient to use a deep electric cooker, which is ideal for the purpose. Moreover, very little preparation is involved—mostly slicing mountains of lamb. Some people skip even that step by asking the butcher to do it for them on a machine.

The Ten-Variety Fire-Pot (No. E 1. below) is such a well-known dish that it is almost a national institution. Counting from bottom layer up, there are celery-cabbage leaves, bean-flour noodles, small pieces of (previously cooked) red-cooked pork and chicken, cooked *tofu*, ground-meat-filled egg wraplings (No. 20.10 of *How to Cook and Eat in Chinese*, except that they are not fried), sliced bamboo shoots (canned if fresh ones are unavailable), half-inch meat balls, and, finally, black mushrooms. When all the layers are in place, clear meat broth is added and the whole pot is brought to a boil in the kitchen before being brought to the table and placed over a low charcoal fire (or electric wok). Then various parts of the contents are served in separate bowls according to individual tastes.

I shall now list some representative Northern dishes. As I have said before, a number of them, like Peking Duck, have long been adopted by Cantonese restaurants and are familiar to American customers. A few are just beginning to make their first appearance in the Western Hemisphere.

A. PASTRIES

点心　　　　*Tien-hsin* literally "dot the heart" (*tien-hsin* is the Northern pronunciation of *tim-sam* in Cantonese. These pastries are usually heavier and bigger than the Cantonese versions.

1. 油條　　*Yu-t'iao*, literally "oily strip" (a kind of long hollow doughnut, but salty rather than sweet)

2. 燒餅　　*Shao-ping*, "sesame biscuits" (a flat bread made partly of short dough, partly of yeast dough, covered with sesame seeds and baked). A daintier, sweeter Shanghai version, called *Ha-k'o-wong* "crab-shell browns," can be found in a few American cities.

3. 春卷儿　*Ch'un-chüar*, "spring rolls" (much like egg rolls and now found almost everywhere, even in TV dinners)

4. 炸餛飩　*Cha Hun-t'un* "fried Won Ton" (another universal favorite found almost everywhere)

5. (大)包子　*Pao-tzu*, or *Ta Pao-tzu* (meat-filled steamed dumpling of raised dough)

6. 小籠包　*Hsiao-lung Pao*, "small steamed dumpling" (a smaller, more elegant version of the above, made with unraised dough; originally a Kiangsu specialty, but now found in Northern restaurants)

7. 花卷儿　*Hua-chüar* "flowery rolls" (steamed rolls, with cross sections like a jelly roll)

8. 餃子　　*Chiao-tzu* "wraplings" (pastry stuffed with meat and vegetables)

9. 鍋貼儿   *Kuo-t'ier,* "pot-sticker" (fried *chiao-tzu*)

B. COLD DISHES

1. 黄瓜凉拌粉皮   Cucumber Strips with Rice Noodles (a salad of cucumbers with a flat kind of rice noodles)

2. 糟鴨肝   Duck Liver with Fermented Sauce

3. 酥魚   *Su Yü* "flaky fish" (fish stewed in soy sauce, vinegar, and scallions until the bones become soft and edible)

4. 糟肉   Meat in Fermented Sauce (In Chekiang Province it is served hot, and becomes a different dish.)

5. 羊膏   *Yang-kao* "lamb cake" (lamb aspic)

6. 糖醋黄瓜   Sweet and Sour Cucumber

7. 虾米拌素菜   Salads of Dried Shrimps and Vegetables

C. STIR-FRY DISHES

1. 軟炸鸡   Soft Fried Chicken (The chicken is cut into serving pieces with the bone left in, then stir-fried with no cornstarch sauce.)

2. 醬爆鸡丁   Stir-Fried Diced Chicken with Bean Paste

3. 糟溜鴨肝   Duck Liver Stir-Fried wtih Fermented Paste

4. 醬汁瓦塊魚   Tile Fish (large pieces of fish,

shaped like pieces of tile, fried with sweet and sour sauce)

5. 炸鳳尾虾　Phoenix Tail Prawns (batter-fried prawns with the tails kept on as decoration)

6. 芙蓉蟹　Crab Fu-yung (crab omelette)

7. 蔥爆羊肉或牛肉　Sliced Lamb or Beef, with Onions

8. 溜黄菜　Thin-Flowing Eggs (a more liquid and runny version of Egg Fu-Yung)

9. 糖醋大魚　Sweet and Sour Whole Fish

10. 油爆尤魚　Oil-Splashed Squid

D. DRY-COOKED DISHES
(no liquid added during cooking process)

1. 乾煎大魚　Dry-Cooked Fish

2. 乾燒冬筍　Dry-Cooked Bamboo Shoots (In America, canned bamboo shoots have to be used, although their taste is not quite ideal.)

3. 虾子鍋揰豆付　Pot-Smeared Bean Curd with Dried Shrimps

4. 鍋燒鴨子　Pot-Braised Duck

5. 乾燒肚子　Dry-Cooked (Pork) Tripe

6. 鷄汁魚肚　Fish Tripe with Chicken Juice

7. 紅扒魚翅　Red-Cooked Shark's Fin (in big clumps, not shreds)

8. 沙鍋魚翅　Sha-Kuo Yü-Ch'ih "sandy pot shark's fin" (A sandy pot is a casserole made of rough-textured unglazed ceramic.)

9. 蔥燒海參　Sea Cucumber with Onions

10. 紅燒大烏參　Red-Cooked Large Sea Cucumbers

11. 水晶肘子　Slow-Cooked Shoulder of Pork

E. FIRE-POT

什錦火鍋　Ten-Variety Fire-Pot (For an example of ingredients see p. 63)

F. SWEETS

1. 炒三泥　Stir-Fried Three Pastes (red, green, and yellow bean purées served together to make a colorful dish)

2. 拔絲蘋果　Pull-Thread Apples (wedges of candied apples served piping hot). With chopsticks, each diner takes a piece and dips it into a bowl of cold water. This cools and hardens the melted sugar coating. The term "pull-thread" refers to the sugar which pulls into thin, long threads.

3. 拔絲山葯　Pull-Thread Sweet Potatoes (same treatment as above)

4. 拔絲香蕉　Pull-Thread Bananas (same treatment as above)

5. 八宝飯　Eight-Jewel Rice (glutinous rice steamed with eight kinds of dried fruits and nuts, such as Chinese dates (jujube), gingko nuts, lotus seeds, purée of beans, etc.)

9

SZECHWAN COOKING

Szechwan food is becoming very fashionable in America. It is quite distinctive in character, and many people, once they get over the initial shock, take to it enthusiastically.

The first thing you can say about Szechwan food is that it is heavily seasoned with hot pepper. An unwary person eating Szechwan food for the first time may think that he has swallowed an exploding firecracker. If you are not used to hot foods, you should tell the waiter in a Szechwan restaurant to go easy on the hot peppers. It's better to suffer a disdainful look from the waiter than to suffer a singed gullet. But if you are willing to take the risk or if you possess an asbestos-lined digestive tract, you will discover that genuine Szechwan food is an eye-opening (as well as eye-watering) experience. More and more people are finding this kind of cooking to their liking, as proved by the rapidly increasing number of Szechwan restaurants.

Szechwan food is not only hot, it is strongly flavored with other seasonings also. One of the preferred methods of cooking is dry-cooking. During this process the food is cooked with some oil and seasoning but little or no additional liquid, so that the flavor becomes very concentrated. Spices and seasonings most often used include hot pepper, black pepper, *Hua-chiao* (*Xanthoxylum piperitum*), star anise, fermented bean paste, black bean paste, wine. It is easy to see why Szechwan dishes are regarded as good rice chasers. Just as American restaurants supply tomato ketchup, a Szechwan restaurant supplies a dish of hot sauce on each table for patrons who want their food even hotter than the way the chef made it. Sweet and sour dishes are also common in Szechwan food, but even in these, hot peppers manage to sneak in. Therefore don't expect a Szechwan Sweet and Sour Fish to taste the same as the Northern or Cantonese versions.

In general, Szechwan cooking is not strong on seafood. The region is landlocked and mountainous, with few navigable rivers and lakes. Even fish ponds are scarce. To make up for the lack of good seafood, Szechwan cooking is unusually rich in ways for preparing vegetables.

Geographically, Hunan is close to Szechwan, and its cooking is sufficiently similar in character so that outside of China these two cuisines are classed together. Within China, however, Hunan cooking holds an honored place by itself. Hunan food makes even more frequent use of hot pepper than Szechwan cooking, and one of my daughters, who was going to school in Hunan, told me that for lunch their main dish was large hot peppers stir-fried with small extra-hot peppers. Examples of Hunan dishes are Dry-Cooked Young Chicken, Dry-Cooked Eel Backs, Diced Chicken with Bean Paste, and Diced Pork—all with hot peppers. The last three are the same as Szechwan dishes Nos. B 1, B 5, and D 3 listed below. But in Hunan custom a jar of extra-hot oil is put on the table in case the diners do not find the seasoning hot enough. Hunan also excels in wind-cured foods. Meat, chicken, fish, etc., are wind-cured and then steamed. Except for wind-cured slices of pork, which one finds once in a long while, the others are rarely found in American Chinese restaurants. As Hunanese cuisine is on the whole similar to Szechwanese, I need not devote a whole chapter to its description.

One of the most famous Szechwan dishes (not counting things like Sour-Hot Soup and Twice-Cooked Meat, which are familiar to all patrons of Mandarin restaurants) is Camphor-Tea Smoked Duck. The recipe for this notable dish is worth giving. First, marinate the duck for at least six hours. (The choice of seasonings depends on your own taste, but they usually include soy sauce, wine, and star anise.) Next, take a large, heavy kettle and place on the bottom some camphor-wood chips (not crystalline camphor!), black tea leaves and dried orange skin. If you cannot get camphor wood, hickory chips will have to do. Then put a metal rack over these materials and place the duck on the rack. Cover tightly and put the kettle over a big fire. Soon smoke will rise from the burning wood chips, tea, and orange skin. If your kettle has a tight lid, the chances are that your neighbor will not call the Fire Department. Let the duck smoke for about fifteen minutes until it acquires a dark-brown color. Then steam the duck until it is half cooked, which takes about half an hour. The last step is to deep-fry the duck for about ten minutes in a big pot of oil until the skin is crisp. You cut up the duck into bite-size pieces and serve it either hot or cold. As you can tell from the recipe, this is not an everyday dish, and not many restaurants are prepared to serve it on short notice.

I shall now list a few typical Szechwan dishes. Many of them are found not only in restaurants that specialize in Szechwan food, but also in restaurants that are styled Mandarin, or Northern. A few of these dishes have even become a regular part of the menu in Cantonese restaurants.

A. COLD DISHES

1. 辣白菜　　Spicy Hot Cabbage (sweet, sour, and hot)

2. 椒麻鸡　　Boiled Chicken with Spiced Sauce

3. 陳皮鸡　　Chicken Spiced with Orange Skin

B. STIR-FRIED DISHES

1. 醬爆鸡丁　Diced Chicken with Bean Paste
   also 　　　(hotter than No. C 2 in the
   called 宮保鸡丁 Northern version)

2. 醬爆肉丁　Diced Pork with Bean Paste

3. 醬爆肉片　　Pork Slices with Bean Paste

4. 辣子鸡丁　　Diced Chicken with Hot Peppers

5. 辣子肉丁　　Diced Pork with Hot Peppers

6. 青椒炒鸡絲　Chicken Shreds with Green Peppers (You can ask for a version with sweet bell peppers if you don't want it too hot.)

7. 耳環尤魚　　Squid Earrings (thin strips of squid, stir-fried so that they curl up and look like earrings)

8. 乾炒牛肉　　Dry Stir-Fried Beef

9. 火爆猪肝　　Stir-Fried Pork Liver

10. 泡菜肉末　　Ground Meat with Pickled Cabbage

11. 螞蟻上樹　　Ants Up a Tree (Not as bad as it might sound: it's ground meat on top of stir-fried bean noodles.)

12. 回鍋肉　　　Twice-Cooked Meat (pork that has been boiled, sliced, and stir-fried with bean paste and hot peppers)

13. 醋溜黄瓜　　Cucumber in Vinegar Sauce

14. 麻鍋豆付　　Bean Curd with Ground Pork, Hot Pepper, and Bean Paste

C. DRY-COOKED DISHES

1. 乾炸明虾　　Dry-Cooked Prawns (with shells on)

2. 黄燜鸡塊　　Braised Chicken

3. 貴妃鸡　　　Chicken Imperial Concubine (Don't get excited, it's chicken.)

4. 子薑鴨塊　Duck with Ginger Sprouts
5. 醋溜黃魚　Kingfish in Vinegar Sauce (The kingfish is not generally available in America, but I once had this dish in a New York restaurant which had imported it from Keemoy.)
6. 糖醋魚　Sweet and Sour Fish
7. 酸辣海參　Sour and Hot Sea Cucumber
8. 乾燒魚翅　Dry-Cooked Shark's Fin
9. 脆皮魚　Crispy Skin Fish

D. STEAMED DISHES

1. 粉蒸鷄　Chicken Steamed with Rice Flour
2. 粉蒸肉　Meat Steamed with Rice Flour
3. 清蒸魚　Steamed Fish

E. SPECIAL DISHES

1. 樟茶鴨　Camphor-Tea Smoked Duck (already described in the introduction to this chapter)
2. 香酥鴨　Fragrant Flaky Duck (A more humble version of the above, the duck is marinated, steamed, and deep-fried until the skin is flaky, somewhat like the skin of the American Southern Fried Chicken.)

10

SOUTHERN DISHES

In the preceding chapters I have described three of the four major cuisines of China. The one that remains to be described is the cooking of south China, namely, the area around the lower parts of the Yangtze valley. Although the region includes Nanking, Shanghai, Hangchow, and many other cities boasting extremely fine cuisines, very few restaurants specializing in Southern cooking are found in America. We who come from this part of China are in the habit of speaking of ourselves as Southerners. Once, I accompanied my husband in his dialect surveys in the real south China, and in Kwangtung, of which Canton is the provincial capital, I found myself saying, "You Cantonese do things this way, we Southerners do them the other way," forgetting that they were the real Southerners and we of the Shanghai-Nanking region were from a place where the British newspaper *North China Daily News* used to be published.

Cantonese cooking has had an early start in America; Northern cooking has snob appeal because Peking is the capital of China; and Szechwan cooking makes an immediate impact with its strong flavors. Lacking these advantages, Southern cooking has been slow to gain recognition in America. Nevertheless, European connoisseurs of Chinese cuisine have long been familiar with Southern cooking. There are several notable Southern Chinese restaurants in Paris and London, for example.

In America, fortunately, some of the more famous Southern dishes can be found in Northern, Szechwan, and Cantonese restaurants. Southern cooking is outstanding in its stir-fried dishes. In fact many of the stir-fried dishes listed in the chapter on Northern food are Southern dishes flavored with a little more salt, soy sauce, or garlic. The Szechwan stir-fried dishes have their Southern counterparts also, only minus the hot peppers.

In flavor, Southern food tends to be on the sweet side. All the dishes that are red-cooked, i.e., stewed with soy sauce, have sugar added to them. In extreme cases, dishes such as Red-Cooked Ham Shanks (*Yuan-t'i*) have so much sugar that the gravy becomes almost syrupy. The taste is not unlike the Japanese teriyaki sauce.

Southern Chinese cooking is unexcelled in fresh-water fish and shrimp dishes, since the region enjoys abundant rivers and lakes. Even Americans who can't name any other Southern dish know about the famous (notorious, rather) dish aptly called Drunken Shrimps, for which Hangchow is well known. After being soaked in strong liquor and seasoning, the shrimps become comatose from the liquor and you are expected to shell and eat the still-wriggling meat, using only your teeth and tongue, without any help from your fingers.

Another Southern Chinese specialty is the Fire-Pot. Of course cooking at the dining table is not a monopoly of this area, or even of China. I have already discussed the Northern Rinsed Lamb at length. In the Southern version, fish, shrimps, scallops, and chicken meat are often added as well as slices of meat. Southerners claim that their Pot is less heavy, less monotonous, and consequently more elegant. One version, the Chrysanthemum Pot, has white chrysanthemum petals added at the end. With the "prehistoric" lazy Susan my father invented years ago, such a pot is within the reach of everybody around the table.

I am not including a list of Southern dishes, because there are few Southern Chinese restaurants as such in America, and because some of the dishes have already appeared in the chapters on Northern and Szechwan food. But I must note one dish I have eaten at a Northern restaurant in America that has its origin in the South, i.e., the Nanking area, and is worth describing. It is called *Chiao-hua Chi* "Beggar's Chicken," and is so named because a beggar would sometimes steal a chicken, drain the blood from its neck, which he would then tuck under its wings, wrap the chicken in thick mud, roast it over burning wood, and after a sufficient length of time, would crack open the mud with a brick or rock—the now dried and hot mud breaking apart would feather the bird automatically. The American Chinese version is to clean the chicken first, wrap it in tin foil, and then bake it in mud in an oven. When it is done, the waiter will present it to you with a hammer, with which you give the first whack, and then he will take the chicken to a side table to do the opening of the chicken and put in the necessary seasonings and then serve the fowl without either mud or tin foil. But recently I have found out that by using three layers of tin foil and adding seasonings after baking, I could bake Beggar's Chicken without any mud, and the result was even better and the procedure simpler and cleaner. For those interested in trying, here are more detailed instructions:

A. SPECIAL DISH

1. 叫化鸡   *Chiao-hua Chi* (Beggar's Chicken) First clean out a 2½-pound or 3-pound chicken. Rub 1 teaspoon salt over the chicken, wrap it in three layers of tin foil, tucking foil also under the wings and legs for better heat conduction. Bake in oven at 450° F. for 2 hours (or 3 hours if larger than 3 pounds). When done, take

out the breastbone for easy access for adding the seasonings: a small can of mushrooms, 3 tablespoons soy sauce (preferably the *sheng-ch'ou* or light-colored kind), 2 teaspoons sugar, 2 scallions cut up (boil these ingredients in a small pot and pour inside the chicken before serving).

11

HOW TO
READ
IN
CHINESE

Now that we have looked over the typical dishes one can order in restaurants of Cantonese, Northern, Szechwan, and Southern types of cooking, it will be useful to know something about Chinese menus, or even to know some of the most frequently occurring Chinese characters—just as it is useful to have a smattering of French for reading American menus, even though the menus in American Chinese restaurants are mostly in bilingual forms.* Here are some of the commonest

* There is no assurance that the bilingual forms translate into each other. Once, in a barbershop in the YMCA in Shanghai, I saw a list of prices of haircuts, shaves, shampoos, etc., and the prices in English were all higher than those in Chinese.—Y.R.C.

Chinese characters that one will meet with in Chinese menus. Of the two forms under each of the Mandarin and the Cantonese pronunciations, the first is what one would most likely find in menus and the second is a near approximation to (American) English.

To be sure, one does not have to know these characters in order to be able to order intelligently, but some familiarity with them will often be of help or at least will impress the waiter favorably.

TABLE OF COMMON CHINESE WORDS IN MENUS

Character	Meaning	Mandarin pronunc.	Like (Am.) English	Cantonese pronunc.	Like (Am.) English
一	one	i	yee	yat	yut
二	two	erh	err	yi	yee
三	three	san	san	saam	psalm
四	four	szu, sze	s + z	sei	say
五	five	wu	woo	ng	(lo)ng
六	six	liu	Leo	luk	look
七	seven	ch'i	chee(se)	ts'at	(i)t's ut (tter)
八	eight	pa	bah	pat	ba(r)t(ender)
九	nine	chiu	Joe	kau	gou(t)
十	ten	shih	shir	sap	sup, sub
元	$	yuan or	you an(d)	yün*	—
(塊,文)	$	k'uai	qui(te)	man	mon(th)

Character	Meaning	Mandarin pronunc.	Like (Am.) English	Cantonese pronunc.	Like (Am.) English
毛	dime	mao	mou(th)	—	—
毫	dime	—	—	hou	ho(se)
水	water	shui	shoe-y	shöi*	shoe-y
火	fire	huo	wha(rf)	fo	fau(cet)
冰	ice	ping	bing	ping	bing
油	oil	yu	yo	yau	yow(l)
盐	salt	yén	yen	yim	yeem (low tone)
醬	bean paste	chiang	jiahng	cheung	jey-ong
醋	vinegar	ts'u	(i)t's oo(ze)	ts'ou	(i)t's oa(ts)
滷	gravy	lu	loo(t)	lou	low
片	slice	p'ien	pian(o)	p'in	pean(ut)
丁	dice	ting	ding	ting	ding
塊	lump	k'uai	quit(te)	faai	figh(t)

皮	skin	p'i	pea	p'ei	pay
心	heart	hsin	sheen	sam	some
絲	shreds	szu	s+z	si	see
餅	cake	pǐng	bing	ping	beng
餃	wrapling	chiao	jow(1)	kau	gou(t)
包	dumpling; to wrap	pao	bou(t)	paau	bou(t)
飯	(boiled) rice; a meal	fan	fan	faan	fa(r)n
粥	congee	chou	jo(ke)	chuk	joke (said with a jerk)
麵	noodles	mien	me an(d)	min	mien
煮	boil	chu	drew	chü	j+ü
蒸	steam	cheng	jun(k)	ching	jing

* There being no ö or ü in English, they are to be pronounced as in German when occurring in forms for Mandarin or Cantonese.—Y.R.C.

Character	Meaning	Mandarin pronunc.	Like (Am.) English	Cantonese pronunc.	Like (Am.) English
燒	cook	shao	shou(t)	shiu	she + you
炒	stir-fry	ch'ao	chow(der)	ch'au	chow(der)
炸	deep-fry	cha	ja(r)	chau	jow(l)
醃	to salt	yēn	yen	yim	yeem (high tone)
牛	ox, cow	niu	new	ngau	(si)ng ou(t)
羊	lamb, sheep	yang	young	yeung	yea-ong
鷄	chicken	chi	jee(p)	kai	guy
鴨	duck	ya	ya(rd)	aap	aap
魚	fish	yü	—	yü	—
肉	meat	jou	roa(d)	yuk	yoke
蝦	shrimp	hsia	sha(rk)	ha	hea(rt)
菜	vegetable; a dish	ts'ai	(i)t's i(ce)	ts'oi	(i)t's oi(l)

素	vegetarian	su	soo(the)	sou	so
大	large	ta	da(rt)	tai	dye
小	small	hsiao	shou(t)	siu	sui(t)
紅	red	hung	hoong	hung	hoong
白	white; plain	pai	by	paak	ba(r)k
甜	sweet	t'ien	tea an(d)	tim	team
酸	sour	suan	so an(d)	sün	—
苦	bitter	k'u	coo(l)	fu	foo(l)
辣	hot (taste)	la	la(rd)	laat	la(r)d
鹹	salty	hsién*	she an(d)	haam	ha(r)m
生	raw	sheng	sh(r)un(k)	saang	—
香	scented	hsiang	she-ah-ng	heung	hay-ong
清	clear	ch'ing	chin(k)	ts'ing	chin(k)

* With a high rising tone, as distinguished from No. 62 below, which has a high level tone.—Y.R.C.

Character	Meaning	Mandarin pronunc.	Like (Am.) English	Cantonese pronunc.	Like (Am.) English
鮮	savory	hsiēn	she-an(d)	sin	seen
鍋	pot	kuo	gour(d)	wo	wa(r)
鑊	cauldron	kuo	gour(d)	wok	walk
盤	plate	p'an	pan	p'un	poon
碗	bowl	wan	w + an	wun	(s)woon
碟	saucer	tieh	dea(r)	tip	dip

EPILOGUE
FOR
THE
EPICURE

Now that you can read some Chinese and order in Chinese, you are ready to eat in Chinese in America.

ABOUT THE AUTHOR

BUWEI YANG CHAO was born in China and is a graduate of Tokyo Women's Medical College. She describes herself as a doctor who "ought to be practicing instead of cooking." A resident of California, she has lived in many parts of China, Europe, and America. She is the author of *How to Cook and Eat in Chinese* (available in Vintage Books).